I0816530

¡Nuestra maravillosa Tierra! / Our Exciting Earth

LAGOS
LAKES

Tanner Billings
Traducido por / Translated by Diana Osorio

Please visit our website, www.garethstevens.com.
For a free color catalog of all our high-quality books, call toll free 1-800-542-2595 or fax 1-877-542-2596.

Library of Congress Cataloging-in-Publication Data
Names: Billings, Tanner, author.
Title: Lagos / Lakes / Tanner Billings.
Description: New York : Gareth Stevens Publishing, 2023. | Series: ¡Nuestra maravillosa Tierra! / Our Exciting Earth | Includes index.
Identifiers: LCCN 2021043387 | ISBN 9781538276112 (library binding) | ISBN 9781538276129 (ebook)
Subjects: LCSH: Lakes–Juvenile literature. | Lake ecology–Juvenile literature.
Classification: LCC GB1603.8 .B55 2023 | DDC 551.48/2–dc23/eng/20211008
LC record available at https://lccn.loc.gov/2021043387

First Edition

Published in 2023 by
Gareth Stevens Publishing
29 East 21st Street
New York, NY 10010

Translator: Diana Osorio
Editor, Spanish: Diana Osorio
Editor, English: Kate Mikoley
Designer: Tanya Dellaccio

Photo credits: Cover Yevhenii Chulovskyi/Shutterstock.com; p. 5 Alicia Garcia Benito/Shutterstock.com; p. 7 Craig Sterken/Shutterstock.com; p. 9 Sergey Novikov/Shutterstock.com; p. 11 bikemp/Shutterstock.com; p. 13 John Brueske/Shutterstock.com; p. 15 Parichat Snguanwongwan/Shutterstock.com; p. 17 Katvic/Shutterstock.com; p. 19 Spiroview Inc/Shutterstock.com; p. 21 Suzanne Tucker/Shutterstock.com; p. 23 Zivica Kerkez/Shutterstock.com.

Printed in the United States of America

CPSIA compliance information: Batch #CSGS23: For further information contact Gareth Stevens, New York, New York at 1-800-542-2595.

Contenido

Contents

Un lago es una gran
masa de agua.
Tiene tierra a
su alrededor.

••••••••••••••••••••••••••••••

A lake is a big
body of water.
It has land around it.

La mayoría son de agua dulce.
Esto significa que no tienen sal.

....

Most have fresh water.
This means no salt.

Algunos lagos tienen sal.
Hay uno en Utah.

....

Some lakes have salt.
Utah has one.

Los ríos van a dar
a los lagos.

••••••••••••••••••••••••••••••

Rivers go into lakes.

Algunos lagos están hechos de hielo.

Some lakes are made by ice.

Parte del agua de
los lagos proviene
de la lluvia.
Otra proviene del suelo.

Some lake water
is from rain.
Some is from the ground!

Los lagos pueden
ser profundos.
Rusia tiene
el más profundo.

....

Lakes can be deep.
Russia has the deepest one.

América del Norte tiene
los Grandes Lagos.
Hay cinco.

....

North America has
the Great Lakes.
There are five.

Puedes nadar en un lago.
También puedes
pasear en bote.

••••••••••••••••••••••••••••••

You can swim in a lake.
You can ride a boat too!

¡Vayamos a un lago!

Let's go to a lake!

Palabras que debes aprender
Words to Know

río/river

agua/water

Índice / Index